Breaking the Cycle

A Journey to My Breakthrough

Prophetess Evangelist Godient A. Kelly-Derbigney

ISBN 979-8-88851-753-6 (Paperback)
ISBN 979-8-88851-754-3 (Digital)

Copyright © 2024 Prophetess Evangelist Godient A. Kelly-Derbigney
All rights reserved
First Edition

All rights reserved. No part of this publication may be reproduced, distributed, or transmitted in any form or by any means, including photocopying, recording, or other electronic or mechanical methods without the prior written permission of the publisher. For permission requests, solicit the publisher via the address below.

Covenant Books
11661 Hwy 707
Murrells Inlet, SC 29576
www.covenantbooks.com

Chapter 1

Being Born into the World

My circle of life began when I was born to my mother, Vivian L. Kelly, and father, Anthony Kelly, on February 26, 1980, in Buffalo, New York. They are veterans who served in the United States Army. They were both stationed in Frankfurt, Germany, which is how my parents met each other. My mother was a private first class stationed at Fort Jackson, South Carolina, for basic training and was a part of Co A 141st Signal Battalion, USAREUR-E7. She was a radio teletype operator.

During her basic training, my mother had to go through the gas chamber. There was a hole in the mask; she had been breathing toxic gas, and they had to remove her. So when the time came to go through the next training course, the sergeant wanted her to jump out of the airplane to receive her airborne badge. She refused. She also faced sexual harassments from her superior officer. He wanted her to go out on a date, and she refused to go on a date. He had her stand guard twenty-four hours in the rain with no relief for refusing. She was soaking wet and caught ammonia. She reported the incident and got it documented.

After the basic training, she was sent to Frankfurt, Germany. She managed to finish serving and received an honorable discharged because of her pregnancy. When my mother was on duty in Frankfurt, Germany, she was assigned to guard the Berlin Wall. My mother's duty was to guard the Berlin Wall and work as a radio operator. Her task was to check for any spy interference over the Satellite Transportable Terminal. She earned a Marksman badge for proficiency with an M-16, making her one of the first females to earn this badge. My father was also a radio operator, and he moonlighted as a DJ in his spare time. My mother participated in model shows and walked the runway. During her time off, she posed for numerous pictures with fellow models. She even took photographs while pregnant with me. I remember one image of her wearing silk pajamas, with her pregnant belly exposed. My mother was a very beautiful woman. She was pregnant with me while serving in the military. She always told me that they wanted to have me and that I was made out of love. After completing their military service, they moved to Buffalo, New York, where my father and his family lived.

My father's family is originally from Columbus, South Carolina, and is of Gullah descent from an African tribe. My mother had to adjust to life in Buffalo as she had no family there and was accustomed to living in Texas. Buffalo is home to many famous people, such as Rick James and Thurman Thomas, a former Buffalo Bills football player. My Aunt Carmela used to be Rick James's hairstylist; she created the braided hairstyle with the bangs that he wore until his passing. Thurman Thomas is my cousin. He also hails from Bay City, Texas. I remember growing up and seeing him visit his mother while he was in college. He used to drive his 5.0 Mustang and would always stop by to visit his cousins Lisa Hall, Maybelline Jones, and me. My mother and I often visited his mother. I used to tease him about his piercings as he was the only person I knew at that time who had two earrings. He gained popularity and started a trend with the two earrings. I am proud of his accomplishments as a famous football player; he has inspired many people to pursue their dreams. He has also contributed to the Buffalo community, helping those in need and encouraging the youth to believe in themselves.

While we were living in Buffalo, a man tried to rob my mother at knifepoint while she was pregnant with me. He told her that if she hadn't been pregnant, he would have hurt her.

It was destined for me to be here. God blessed them with a beautiful little girl. I had my struggles when I was born. Sickness had attacked my fragile little body. When I was born, I was two pounds and two ounces. I was premature and couldn't breathe due to lack of oxygen. I was also diagnosed with asthma. The doctor told my parents I wasn't going to make it because of the difficulty breathing and I was slipping into a coma due to the lack of oxygen. Doctors suggested various surgeries such as tracheostomy. Tracheostomy is performed when your airway is blocked or when a disease makes breathing impossible. The thought of having to live with a tube through my throat and struggling to talk caused concerns. Also, my lung could've collapsed if I needed to have the tracheostomy permanently. The doctor also said that if I survive, I would have problems talking and walking.

My mother went to the chapel at the hospital and prayed to God to save my life. While my mother was praying, my father was in the room watching over me and praying too. I was their only child at the time, and they knew God wouldn't put more on them than they could bear. God came to my mother with a name to give me and said, "I will save her." At that moment, the doctors came to get her and to tell her that they don't know what happened, but I was doing better, and it was a miracle that I was still alive without the surgery. My mother told the doctor that it was God and that "I'm naming my daughter *Godient Antoinette Kelly*." At first, my parents wanted to name me *Antoinette* after my father, which turned out to be my middle name. However, God had a calling on my life; God came to my mother and told her to name me *Godient*. My name carries a meaning, and I was always constantly asked, "What does it mean?" So I will tell people that it means to always put God first in all of my decisions and keep God in my life. Never leave your life totally in the doctor's hands and going by the diagnosis the doctor gives you. Always go to God. He is the head of your decision-making and should be included in every aspect of your life. I was able to live my life without any of the problems that the doctor said I would have. That is why I believe in the Lord, and He is my Savior.

As I lived on, I've learned the importance of me being here in this world and to use my name to always remember the true meaning of my purpose in life. The first three letters of my name are *G-O-*

D, which spells out *God*. This gives me the purpose to keep telling people that I come across the meaning and for them to know the person that God called me to be. Furthermore, for other individuals to know who I live for, which is Jesus. Some people that I came across were delighted and smiled when I told them my name. They understood the meaning of it, and then I had some that didn't have the true understanding of what God has called me to be. I have been mistreated and disrespected. During those times, I was young but still able to take the sense to know these individuals will not be included in my life very long.

I lived my life as a normal child and as a regular person. I made some choices that might not have been the best. Without those choices, I might have never known and learned about the hardship that you receive when you make decisions that are not pleasing to God. When we lived in Buffalo, we used to always be with my father's family. My Aunt Carmela told me that I used to stay in the middle of the floor as a baby, and I would sing like no one was there. I don't know how I was sounding then, but I know it was beautiful. My Aunt Carmela used to braid my hair a lot. I loved shaking my hair because I had beads in the front of my bangs. As time went by, my mother was ready to move back to Texas because she missed her family. She decided to move to Houston, Texas.

In the next chapter of my life, God had blessed us with an angel named Eboni Nicole Kelly. Eboni was born on February 19, 1983, in Houston, Texas, at Texas Children's Hospital. My mother raised us to be close. She always told me to love her and treat her as if she were my little girl. I would tell my mother that I would always protect her. We didn't know that the time we had with Eboni was going to be short-lived. My parents found out at the age of two that Eboni had Yatu cancer. It was a rare cancer of the tailbone.

One day, when my grandmother Perlin Kelly was watching Eboni, she noticed that every time Eboni had to sit down, she would fall over and cry. My grandmother called my parents to tell them they needed to come back to New York to find out what was wrong with her. My parents brought her back to Houston and took her to Texas Children's Hospital. They had to stay in the Ronald McDonald

House at Texas Children's Hospital in Houston, Texas. The doctors told them they had to stay there with her because she needed various chemo treatments. The doctors told them the side effects of the treatment, like feeling fatigue and the loss of her thick, beautiful hair. They called her the "Sunshine Kid" because she would always smile and had a glow. The hospital staff took pictures of her with the rest of the children who had to stay at the Ronald McDonald House. She still managed to be happy. My parents took turns being at the hospital.

I remember visiting her for a little while. I couldn't stay overnight because I was five years old at the time. When I got home, I would miss her and cry because I wanted her to come home. My parents came home one day and had to tell me that she wasn't coming back home because she had gone to heaven. At the time, I didn't understand why she had to go and why she didn't get better. At that moment, I realized how much I missed her and that I was going to grow up without her. I kept every picture of her in my room to get through the pain. Sometimes I would cry when I saw her pictures. My parents told me she was in a better place and didn't have to suffer anymore and that God needed her in heaven. Now that I'm grown, I understand why He took her. He took her instead of me because He had a purpose for me to fulfill and deliver His Word. Also, she was the angel He needed. When we had Eboni's funeral, we had it in Cedar Lane, Texas. It was hard on the family to see her leave so soon. My mother decided to sing her last song to her. It was called "Goin' Up Yonder" by Tramaine Hawkins. She sang the song with poise and strength. When she sang the song, she added Eboni's name to it. It was hard for her having to deal with the loss of Eboni.

After the funeral, it hit her really hard. She had a lot of emotions because her baby had passed away, and after the funeral, things weren't in order as they should've been, which had her stressed out and upset. There was nothing prepared at my grandmother's house during the funeral, which left an embarrassing impression because the guests were arriving and the house wasn't clean and presentable. She had to clean up the house to have dinner for the guests. Instead of her family being there at a time of bereavement to help and assist with cleaning the home for the funeral, she found her way to make it through the funeral and deal with her passing. After my sister's passing, my mother stayed more involved with me by entering us in a singing contest. We sang "He's Got the Whole World in His Hands." We won first place. I had a chance to take a picture with my trophy sitting in a wicker chair. My cousin Opal was with us, and we took a picture together. My mother kept me singing to every one of her friends to give me confidence to be able to sing in front of everyone. My mother and I were close. I was always with her all the time.

Chapter 2

Remembering the Evil in This World

We lived in the poorest part of Houston, which was McGowen Street in the Third Ward District. We moved there because we had just moved from Buffalo, New York. It was a place to stay until my parents could afford a better place to stay. It kind of reminded me of *Brewster Place*, the TV show with Oprah Winfrey living in a poor neighborhood with a wall blocking the other side. That wall created a haven for drug dealers, drunks, and prostitutes. The neighborhood that we lived in had the same thing: it had a dead-end road that was blocked with a whole lot of trash, and people would illegally dump trash there. We used to sit out on the front porch sometimes, and my mother would be talking to her friends. My mom would press my hair outside, or sometimes she would braid it. I was a rough little girl, but my mother always kept me beautiful with my bows and barrettes. She would have a bucket of my hair barrettes in a plastic tub.

My parents were close to some of the people in the neighborhood. My mother had a friend named Daisy; she stayed across the street from us in an upstairs apartment with her daughter. Sometimes they would have parties and play cards outside. The kids will play outside. One day one of the neighbors invited my parents to a party. They were outside playing cards. They told my parents that it was okay for me to sleep in one of the rooms while they were playing cards. There was no one in the room at the time. I woke up, and I saw a man on top of me touching me in the most inappropriate places; he was touching my vagina. I hollered and screamed for my dad. My dad came in just in time before he could finish molesting and raping me. I was a baby, three to four years old, and I remember like it was yesterday. My mother screamed, and my father fought the man and his family. The whole neighborhood was outside. The cops came and arrested him. He was locked up for a long time. He never could return to that neighborhood for what he had done. Neighbors were wondering if there was anybody else that he molested or raped. Satan was trying to take my innocence away to make me emotional and mentally bound.

As I got older, my parents taught me everything about not talking to strangers: never get too close to an adult and never let them touch you sexually. My parents tried to avoid all those things, but Satan managed to creep in that man. They were just playing cards and putting their trust on people whom they thought they knew, not imagining that someone in their family could be a sick pedophile. I have never told anyone this because I didn't want to be looked at as a victim and leave myself to be vulnerable to anyone. I stressed to my kids that evil and sickness hides in people. You can't see it until you are alone.

Predators have a symptom of always wanting to get kids by themselves. For instance, in Alabama, there was a child name Kamille "Cupcake" McKinney and another little baby who were kidnapped by Patrick Stallworth and his girlfriend Derick Brown. Patrick Stallworth was on video kidnapping and luring the babies with candy at a birthday party that took place at a family's/friend's home at a Tom Brown Park housing project in Birmingham, Alabama. The children were left outside unattended in the evening for countless of hours, and it was dark outside. There was no one outside with them. Kamille was raped, drugged, and killed. They left her body in a landfill. She was someone's child, and she was loved. I can't imagine how she was feeling in her last moment.

There is a video showing Kamille riding her bike for the last time smiling with her mother before she went to the party. She looked happy and excited. There is a statement by Derick Brown stating that she saw Patrick Stallworth kneel down with her performing sexual acts with her. Before Kamille's disappearance, Patrick Stallworth was released from jail for child pornography, and Derrick was released from jail for kidnapping her own children by gunpoint at a foster home after losing custody. They deserve the justice that they are about to get because they just got of jail for child pornography and holding children at gunpoint. They even tried to give an older child on the same day candy too. They had told the young girl that was looking for a girl like her. Thank God they didn't kidnap her too. They should have never been released from jail.

The problem with pedophiles is they don't stay in jail long enough, and it is possible that they will commit the same crime. We need to create stiffer laws for pedophiles. We should post their face on billboards or create a pedophile video alert on the highways like an AMBER Alert or the news the moment they are released from jail. A notification by mail doesn't work because sometimes they aren't even registered as a sex offenders, and sometimes you are not notified by mail to let you know that they have been released, especially if you have been victimized by them. Maybe that will deter them from committing a crime. Before 1996, there was no Megan's Law, which is a database for registered sex offenders to give information on where they live. Megan's Law exists because of a seven-year-old girl who was murdered and raped by her neighbors. Also they needed to create a device that they can't remove for the extent of their life span. You can't trust people to the fullest extent because you don't know what they are capable of.

When you have young children, especially babies, it is best for you to watch them and keep them close as much as you can. Remind your children that it is okay to tell you when someone hurts them, no matter who it is. You should listen to your children and watch their demeanor. Single mothers should never leave their children with their boyfriend or husband. It doesn't matter how much you think you know them; some men tend to treat your children differently when you are not there. Some people like to portray themselves a certain way around people whom they don't want knowing about who they truly are. It doesn't matter what gender your child is; predators will take advantage of them just the same. There are women too who seek young boys, especially when they are getting older and about to be an adult.

Watch for those comments that some people make sometimes ("You can be my boyfriend or girlfriend") because it just might not be a joke. Sometimes people will say it as a joke, but who in their right mind wants to mess with a young child? Sometimes you have to wonder even when they are grown. You will find yourself being taken advantage of when you are feeling weak and vulnerable. People will take advantage of your situation to show you who they really are. Their eyes don't lie. Your facial expressions and body language around a person say a lot.

Never blame the child. Always press charges. Speak for other victims. You are not just helping yourself; you are helping other people from getting victimized. If you see a child in harm's way, help them and report it because children are defenseless. Children can remember from the age of three. Even though this happened to me many years ago, I felt like I was responsible for helping keep someone else from being a victim. If someone sexually abuses your child, never look at yourself as the person who couldn't save them. It is Satan trying to get you to play the blame game. You can't be with your children 24-7. We have our prayers and God. God was still with me that night. My Father up above came right on time. I also thank my dad for being my hero.

Chapter 3

Going through Emotional and Financial Hardship with My Parents

After my sister's passing, we had to move out of our home because my parents had to use the majority of their money on Eboni's medical bills and her funeral. We had nowhere to go. We were living out of our truck, and it got really cold one night. We snuck inside an office building where my father had worked. We slept there for the night. Sometimes we slept outside my father's job. He would park the truck until it was time for him to go to work; then my mother would take the truck for the rest of the day. My father was still working as a security officer. He sacrificed his job for us to make sure we weren't freezing in the truck. However, we still didn't have enough money to move right away, so we had to stay in our truck most of the time until my family found another place to stay.

During that time, the hardship and the passing of my sister were testing my parents' marriage. My mother had to go out and get two jobs; plus she went to school. My father applied at the Veteran Hospital. They hired him right away because he was an army veteran. Later, he took on a second job at the *Houston Chronicle*. My father is a great man and proud. He did all he could to take care of us. I always looked at him as an example of how a man should be. He always taught me that a man should do whatever he can to take care of his family. A man should work two jobs before a woman does. A man should show love toward his woman without being ashamed. A family builds a man's character. Nothing should come between him and his wife.

My mother believed in the Lord; she was the prayer warrior in the family. She was saved and accepted the Lord at the age of thirteen. I remember when we used to go to church at people's homes; church was not just in a building—it was outside and at home. Eventually, one of the people we had church with was able to get their own church. She kept me in church. As I got older, I even went by myself when my mother got sick. That taught me she wanted me to stay in church no matter what, even if she wasn't there because, as I would get old, I would never depart from Him. As it says in Proverbs 22:6 (KJV): "Train up a child in the way he should go: And when he is old, he will not depart from it."

I always had to tell her what the pastor's sermon was about. Then we would talk about it later. She kept me active in the choir and drill team. She also gave me a stern, military-style discipline. She taught me how to do things the right way the first time; if not, I would have to do it all over again, like cleaning my room, washing dishes, and taking care of my hygiene. If the dishes weren't clean enough, she would take them out of the cupboard and make me wash them all over again. She used to wake me up from my sleep to wash the dishes over, and I'd better not have said anything. It taught me how to do things correctly and to take her seriously with a lot of respect.

I remember when my parents started to have marriage problems, and they would argue. Sometimes they would fight. I saw my mother hurting and crying. There were things I should never have witnessed, like her being dragged in the hallway and beaten with a belt like she was a child. Then he burnt her on her breast with an iron. My mother and I went to the hospital where they had to bandage her breast with a compress bandage. My Aunt Mary came to get us when the fights worsened. I would seek refuge in my neighbor's home or friends' home to get away from the fighting. One time, I snuck out of the window at the age of seven; no one could find me until my friend's mother brought me home. Then my mother had to finally to speak out and tell someone what was going on. My mother even got arrested because my father was supposed to pick me up from school one day. She had thought he had picked me up, but he didn't. I had to wait outside with the teacher, then Houston police had escorted me home. When they arrived, my mother was furious at my father for not picking me up. No one was in trouble until she felt offended; she felt the officers were trying to accuse her of not picking me up from school. She kept telling them that my farther was supposed to get me from school. All I remember was her being on the ground. They had put handcuffs on her ankles so she couldn't move. They arrested her for an assault on a police officer. They gave her a misdemeanor. She was released the next day. That was when she told me to never depend on a man to watch your child. My mother couldn't take it anymore, so we stayed with my Aunt Mary for a while. However, they got back together. They even went to the pastor of our church at New Life Baptist Church together for counseling.

My father rededicated his life to the Lord. It was my first time seeing my father receive the Holy Ghost. He was standing at the altar with Pastor Perry while he was praying for him. He was crying, and saliva was coming out of his mouth. I was nine and asked my mother, "What is the Holy Ghost, and why is my father spitting out of his mouth? What does it mean?" She told me it was the Holy Spirit working within him and that sometimes you can speak in tongues. It is a gift from God and a way to praise God. Sometimes, if you have impure spirits in you, they will be cast out of you. My parents stayed married for fourteen years, until 1990. My mother decided to get a divorce because of infidelity reasons. As a child, I had witnessed my father commit adultery. At that moment, it was more than she could handle. She felt like her dignity, pride, and womanhood were being attacked. The mistress didn't have any respect for herself. She did some things that were out of line, like calling her and hanging up on her.

This happened on the day I was supposed to meet my father for visitation. I went to McDonald's on my bike to meet him, but he never showed up. That was the first time I was ever disappointed by my father. I rode my bike all the way home crying. I left my bike outside downstairs from our apartment. When I came back outside, my bike was stolen. I was hurt. First, my father wasn't there at McDonald's to see me, and then my bike was stolen—all in the same day. My mother and her best friend were upset because I was let down by my father for the first time, and my bike was stolen. They decided to take me shopping at the Gulfgate Mall to lift my spirits. My mother's friend used her credit card and bought me a beautiful dress. That dress became my favorite dress. I couldn't stop thanking her and gave her a hug. She looked at me that day and told me to remember that I'm always loved. She also told me to walk with my head up and always know that I'm beautiful, no matter what someone might tell me.

My mother bought me another bike with her rent money. I was delighted and happy. We returned home from shopping. There was no call from my father that night. The next day, my mother received another phone call from my father's mistress asking about me. I overheard my mother telling her not to call anymore and that the only person who needed to be calling was my father so he could explain himself to his daughter. While my father stayed with that woman, I saw how a man can lose his values and his self-worth for another woman.

One night he came by the house, and somehow an argument started. He barged into our home and took all my mother's money. He stormed outside with that woman downstairs, yelling things at my mother. My mother was chasing after my father to get her money back. She didn't win that fight, but she got the money back and then some later on in the years after she had passed away. The other woman turned him into a man that I was not proud of. She did a lot of childish and bold things that some women will do to break up a home and to try to make you angry. After that, she even dropped my father off where we lived when she was told to stay off the property where we lived. My Uncle Henry had to witness all of this.

In today's age, we call them side chicks. That is why they are called side chicks and mistresses. However, in biblical terms, a whore, harlot, courtesan, or a prostitute means to have unlawful sexual commerce, to practice lewdness (KJV dictionary definition). They will do all things to upset the wife. They will never be the wife or take the place of the wife because they are together in sin. They are sinning together. Eventually, in due time, that man will have to give account for what he has done because he has committed adultery. Your flesh will be tested, and it is weak. Even though you mean to do the right things, sometimes you are faced with temptation. *Temptation* is the desire to do something, especially something wrong or unwise (*Oxford Languages*) to see if you can restrain from things that you are not supposed to have or do. You will be tempted to see if you can be faithful and stay true to the one you gave vows to under God. Furthermore, Satan doesn't like togetherness under holy matrimony and will do anything to destroy the marriage.

Life tends to look better on the other side. However, you are just being blind to the consequence of committing adultery. If a woman commits adultery and lies, she will be cursed by her husband. There are many consequences like having an illegitimate child outside of your marriage, diseases, being used for money, and being set up. You also can lose your family and the things that you got together as a family. Oh yes, there are people who are willing to break up your marriage because they're jealous of you having a chance to have a prosperous marriage and obviously have a motive. Most individuals know that no good comes from breaking up a marriage by being with them while they're married because the husband and wife made a vow to each other under God to stay together. You have to think twice before you step outside your marriage or into someone else's marriage because you will be held accountable. Matthew 5:28 (KJV) says, "But I say unto you, That whosoever looketh on a woman to lust after her hath committed adultery with her already in his heart." Hebrews (KJV) states, "Marriage is honorable in all, and the bed undefiled: but whoremongers and adulterers God will judge." Even if they are separated, he/she is still obligated to stay faithful because you are still legally married. It is known as putting away a wife or husband.

Many scriptures reference adultery in divorce and separation:

> Whosoever putteth away his wife and marrieth another, committeth adultery: and whosoever marrieth her that is put away from her husband committeth adultery. (Luke 16:18)

> And unto the married I command, yet not I but the Lord, Let not the wife depart from her husband. (1 Corinthians 7:10–11)

> But if the unbelieving depart, let him depart. A brother or a sister is not under bondage in such cases: but God hath called us to peace. (1 Corinthians 7:15)

During separation, it is the time to recollect your thoughts and figure out how you can grow in your marriage. Your vows are not just words, and your marriage license is not just a paper.

When God sends you someone to marry, you are marrying someone like Him, or He can send you someone who is a whore, like He did Hosea, to portray a message of repentance to God's people. God has to truly send you someone, and you shouldn't try to find someone on your own because you might find someone who is not of God and God-fearing. However, God does give you the free will to choose. I prefer God's helping hand. People tend to wear many disguises, and you can easily be tricked with looks, money, property, sex, and anything that you think you are lacking at home. However, you can have all those things in your marriage if you take time and invest in the one you made vows to.

Couples who stayed together for fifty years and more didn't stay together without any trials. All marriages that look perfect have gone through some kind of affliction any time when you are doing something that God seeks favor in. Sometimes the devil will test you. He will test you in your faith, marriage, and relationships (family, friends, coworkers, etc.). I was at the divorce proceedings when my parents got divorced. The judge ordered my parents to get me counseling because it is hard for a child to see their parents get a divorce. Sometimes kids feel like it is something that they did. At the end of the proceedings, I cried so hard and tried to go with my father. I was holding on to my father's hand so tight until it started to slip away. I didn't want them to get a divorce. However, my dad left, and I was hurt. I was upset at the two of them.

I started having problems in school. My mother had a teacher/parent conference with one of my teachers named Mrs. Oliskey from Askew Elementary. Mrs. Oliskey was a wonderful teacher. She understood me and helped my mother get through our problems. I started taking my counseling sessions at school. Later on, my father told me that he didn't want to see me cry, and I was better off with my mother at the time. He told me that she will need me and to help her. I was able to see him every other weekend. I was always looking forward to those weekends. He would always take me shopping. We would go out to places like Astroworld and Fame City, which is Funplex now. The relationship between my parents after the divorce was better. My father wasn't with his mistress anymore, and the distance we had due to him being with her helped them to be better friends and coparents.

As I got older, I started to realize that I will face many obstacles and trials in life. I will have disappointments, but I have to move forward and make my decisions for myself in who I decide to let in my life and let go. My father taught me as a man that they make mistakes, and we have to step back to let them understand what mistake they had made. My mother always made sure I had a relationship with my father, and he always stayed involved in my life. She always spoke positively about him and told me to always respect him in spite of. She always made sure that when I misbehaved, he was just a phone call away and he was on his way to see why I was misbehaving.

Chapter 4

Life after My Parents' Divorce

After the divorce, my mother wanted a fresh start, so we moved to Bay City, Texas, where my mother was born and raised. When we moved to Bay City, I had to get used to the small country town. We used to always come and visit my mother's side of the family in Bay City on the weekends. However, it was actually different having to live there. I had to adjust because I was raised in Houston at the time, and there was more to do there. However, everyone knows everybody, and you are related to the majority of the people in the town. People will wave or honk their horn like they knew you already. I used to ask my mother why people were always waving at us. I would tell her that we don't know them. She would tell me to wave anyway because it is polite to wave back, and eventually we will know who they are.

The move to Bay City gave me a chance to get to know more of my mother's side of the family besides her immediate family. We used to go to my cousin Nancy's house all the time, and I would play with her daughters. We would go to baseball games, play volleyball at her house, or at the park. We also would sit outside talking, laughing, and having a good time. If we weren't at Nancy's house, we would be spending time with my Grandfather Moses Bree, who would come by and have dinner with us. My grandfather was born to Henry Bree and Dellie Bree. He stayed in church, and he would always sing. He sang at almost every church in Matagorda County. He was known for his baritone voice singing his solos. His favorite song he would sing was "Precious Lord." He was married to my grandmother Ruby Mae White Bree. My grandmother Ruby's parents were Daniel White and Marnirva Taylor. My grandmother was sixteen years old when they got married and already had a child, which was my uncle Roy. Then she had my aunt Mary, uncle Leo, uncle Henry, aunt Leslie, uncle Moses, my mother Vivian, and at last my aunt Karen.

My great-grandmother Marnirva was killed by a man named Henry Hicks. She was having an affair with him. My grandfather Moses had found her and saw the man who killed her. After my great-grandmother's death, my great-grandfather Daniel left his children when she died. My great-grandfather went to drop off his younger children who were still living with him at my grandparents', but my grandfather Moses didn't want them to stay with them. My great-grandfather moved to Houston and moved back when he was sick. He moved in with his daughter Jessie Powell, who is my great-aunt. Aunt Jessie and her daughter Willamae Gean Gatson helped take care of him and the rest of the siblings.

Growing up, my grandmother Ruby Mae White would take all of her grandchildren to church with her, and we stayed in church all day. My grandparents were separated at the time, but my grandfather would go and visit her. He would sing and talk until it was time to go home. He could never go a day without her. Some people would say he was stubborn and mean sometimes. He did some mean things, like when my mother was a child, he was fighting with my grandmother, and my mother had tried to stop the fight by hitting him in his back. My grandfather threw a crowbar at her as she was running out of the house. The crowbar missed her by an inch. He also made my uncle Moses carry bricks around the house when he did something wrong.

Uncle Roy one day came in the house and hit my grandfather in the back of the head while he was shaving in the bathroom. My grandfather was cussing him out. He pulled up his pants and pulled out his gun. He started shooting at Uncle Roy all the way until he was out in the streets. He came close to almost killing him. Uncle Roy had hit him because he was told that my grandfather was beating on my grandmother. She was his only parent, and he was defending her.

However, it almost got him killed. Some family members say Uncle Roy was treated differently because he wasn't his biological son. As a child, I saw a sweet, lonely man. My grandfather was unkind to my grandmother and abusive to the children while they were married. I can tell you that he felt guilty for his actions because he would go to her house and ask her to come back home. She would say no. It was sad sometimes to watch him go to his house that was falling apart. We still loved him.

We tried on many occasions to help him, but he would refuse our help. His children and grandchildren would still go by the house to check on him. He would tell us stories about his past and how he met my grandmother. We all stayed and listened to him. My grandmother's health was deteriorating, and she had to move out of her house that she shared with my Uncle Leo to go live with my aunt Leslie until she passed away in 1990. We took her passing hard because she helped raise some of us, and we loved her a lot. She kept all of us in church. We stayed in church every Sunday until the second service had ended. We would go home with her until each of our parents came to pick us up to go home with them. My grandfather continued to live on his own in his house alone until he passed away.

Through my teenage years, my mother decided to move to San Antonio in 1993, where my aunt Karen lived. She told my mother there were better opportunities in San Antonio than in Bay City, Texas. When we moved to San Antonio, we stayed in one of the notorious neighborhoods on the Eastside of San Antonio. They used to call it the Shootout Corral, a.k.a. the Wheatley Courts Apartments. We stayed with my aunt Karen until we had our own apartment in the same apartment complex. We didn't live there long because there were a lot of people getting killed there. It wasn't safe. I couldn't play outside like a normal kid. The majority of the time, we had to sleep in the living room. Sometimes we had to sleep on the floor because our room had a window that was facing toward the alley, and many people would drive on that road to do a drive-by or to get away from someone shooting at them.

On our first night moving into our apartment, someone was killed. We went to the store to buy some food for the house. The store was located on the apartment complex and called Malik's. On the way back, we heard gunshots. People were scattering around; I was scared because we had never lived in a neighborhood where you heard gunshots that close. People were crying, and the police sirens were wailing, and ambulance lights were flashing. We couldn't get to our apartment because it was blocked off; someone was shot and killed. We saw that it was a man and a pregnant woman in their car who were shot. It seemed that someone had shot them while they were sitting in their car. The man was shot in his neck and pronounced dead. The woman was shot; I don't know if she made it. The neighborhood was known for gang activities. I wanted to move the moment we moved in, but we had just moved in. I managed to stay out of gangs by staying active in school activities and going to church. I stayed around people who weren't in a gang. If it wasn't for my mother and her character, I would've been lost and misguided. She stood up for me and was my best friend.

The store owner of Malik's came to know my mother and respected her because she was a good mother to me. He would always call her "Mom" instead of calling her by her name. That was his way of saying he liked her because he came across all kinds of people and felt that a lot of the kids in the neighborhood could have a chance if they had good parents and good role models. He kept a lot of pictures of the people he cared for on his wall by the register in his store. Tonya and I were up on that wall. My mother made sure I wasn't out on the streets late at night, and I kept close with my cousin Tonya. Tonya and I would go to the store called Muhammed, which was owned by a Muslim. They had a restaurant in the back, and you could play pool. Everyone went there and felt safe. You could play music on the jukebox and play a game of pool. Even my mother came in there a couple of times and played some of her favorite music. Mother loved to play Betty White's "After the Pain" on the jukebox.

Tonya and I also would go to the malls and the River Walk sometimes to have fun. If I wasn't with her, I was with some of my friends from school. I literally had to be in by six o'clock because around that time it would be dark outside, and that was when a lot of the violence would start most of the time. It's sad that you can't walk through your own neighborhood without someone trying to see if you are a gang member or a rival gang member. You had to be very careful about what colors you were wearing; mainly, if you were wearing a bandana flag, they would threaten or kill you. Tonya and I grew up in a small town and didn't have to worry about what color to wear. We were kids, and our parents raised us as Christians. I'm sure there were other people who lived there too just like us. It was their circumstance that caused them to live in a poor and gang-territory environment. One lady got stabbed in the middle of the day. A man also got killed at the bottom of the stairs of my aunt Karen's apartment.

One summer I went to stay the summer with my father at my father's home. When I came back, my mother told me that there was a man who had gotten into an altercation with someone. He had gone back walking through the neighborhood on N. Mittman Street with a machine gun because some guys had jumped on him and beaten him pretty badly. After that, various fights started to break out. I was glad that she was okay and she wasn't hurt. There was no denying that I had grown up in the hood.

One day my mother and I got sick at the same time. We had to go to the hospital in an ambulance. We had different rooms. I had to share my room with a victim who was bitten by a pit bull. There were news reporters everywhere. Our room was on lockdown, and we couldn't speak to anyone. After being released, we had to call a cab to go home. When the cab driver asked where we were going, he said, "Oh no, I cannot take you there," but my mother pleaded with him. He said, "I can drop you off around the corner, but I can't drive up into those apartments. Sorry, it is horrible over there." We laughed because we understood and also knew he wasn't the only cab driver who felt that way. It was hard getting a cab. When we needed to go somewhere, we had to catch the bus. However, everyone who lives in housing apartments are not bad people; they are just looking for a way out and deserve to live in a better environment so they can have a future for themselves and their children. For instance, my mother wanted a better life for us, and she decided to go back to college and attended St. Phillips College. She kept me around that kind of environment so I could know that I could achieve my goals and get out of poverty.

    We would go to plays with a fellow colleague of hers and other events that were taking place at the college. I also kept myself busy by joining the school choir at Wheatley Middle School. We had the best choir. Our choir director would teach each choir member individually how to train our voices and to sing from our diaphragm. We would go on field trips to other schools and churches to be in a contest. I had a solo, and I won second place. I was happy with second place because I was getting sick and hoarse. I still managed to sing great. When I turned fourteen years old, I had applied for a summer job with BOIC. It was a summer program for teenagers to learn how to apply for a job and work. I was working at Sam Houston High School. I attended classes and worked in the office. I still managed to become a person with a promising future. I had met a couple of colleagues who managed to go to the same college as I did, who either were from the same apartments or lived in other housing apartments. We stayed for a while until I reached the eighth grade and graduated from Wheatley Middle School.

    Eventually, the City of San Antonio tore the apartments down and built affordable luxury apartments, which are now called East Meadows. The summer of '95, my father helped us move back to Houston, Texas. We lived with my aunt Mary for a little while. I attended M. B. Smiley my freshman year. I met a lot of superstars there. It was a great school. I went there when Calvin Murphy's daughter was going there. A lot of hip-hop stars and R&B singers like Jodeci had performed at the school during our pep rallies, and the coach used to play all of the Gap Band songs over the intercom. In the cafeteria, there were local rappers who became famous, like Slim Thug, who did rap battles every day at the lunch table for fun. I was the shy one, standing by and watching them rap. I met some new friends. I even started a singing group, and I even started my craft in songwriting. The singing group didn't get a chance to develop because of the members in the group, and I had to move again back to Bay City.

PROPHETESS EVANGELIST GODIENT A. KELLY-DERBIGNEY

When we moved back, my mother had it on her heart to move back to her father's home, but it was condemned. The city of Bay City wouldn't allow her to renovate the house because it wasn't fixable. With so much neglect done to the home, we couldn't save it. Eventually, the house got demolished, and there is just nothing there but an empty lot. We moved into our own apartment after we found out that we couldn't stay in my grandfather's house.

When we moved back to Bay City, it wasn't a great feeling for me because I was getting used to the school that I was already in, and it was on my birthday when we had to move. I was starting to become my own person. I was finally enjoying being a teenager. Being in high school is hard, and making friends was not easy. However, the move back to Bay City for my mother was hard. She continued to raise me as an independent woman, and I grew up to be a mature young adult. I had my second job at the Bay Cinema 4 movie theater. I would go to school and work. The first paycheck I had, I went and bought my mother an outfit. I even helped pay some of the bills. That was the first time I ever paid a bill. This made me happy because I loved my mom, and there wasn't anything I wouldn't do for her.

When I was in high school, my mother's health was deteriorating due to emphysema, diabetes, and asthma. My managers at the time, Jill and Gina, were godsent. I'm grateful that He sent them to me because they helped me through the time I had to work and be there for my mother. God blessed me and my mother to be able to have great times together. We went to concerts and traveled together. We went to see Prince perform in a concert. We also saw Mary J. Blige, Dru Hill, and Ginuwine. I also took a picture with Ginuwine at the concert. I managed to run into a classmate of mine while we were there. We enjoyed the concert together. We drove out of town to go see my uncle Leo, who is blind, in Palacios, Texas. I drove all the way there and back.

I was even blessed to go to my prom, and my mother was there to see me go to my prom with my friends. I almost didn't go to my prom because my date didn't show up to pick me up, but my mother encouraged me to go anyway. I learned at that moment to never let anything get in the way of me being happy and enjoying every moment of my life. I went to my prom in a cab and joined the rest of my friends there. I ended up enjoying myself to the fullest. My date, who was supposed to pick me up, brought me home, and we chilled for the rest of the day. I was so glad that I had gone because if I hadn't attended my prom, I probably would have regretted it, and my mother was able to see me go to my prom.

One week later after prom, on April 21, 1999, that was the day I received my graduation gown. I was so excited to show my mother my gown so I could try it on for her. When I returned home, she had passed away. I found her dead in a hotel where we were staying due to an eviction we had from the previous apartment we lived in. This took place a week after prom. We had received a notice to vacate our apartment due to a balance being owed; however, a lot of it had to do with the living conditions of the apartment complex and complaints to the manager about the appliances that needed to be replaced. My mother was taking insulin that needed to be refrigerated in a working refrigerator. The refrigerator was in such bad condition that mice would get in. The manager replaced the refrigerator for us and placed us in another apartment that had an air-conditioner. My mother wasn't able to continue to pay the rent, and it wasn't announced to me that we had a balance because I would have helped.

The manager decided to evict us, and we had to move into a hotel. Before I left school on that day, I remember it was the day of the Columbine shooting. My mother was taking a shower and stressing about our situation. It was hard losing our place of residence when all she wanted was a better living situation for us and to be stable in her hometown. She always wanted me to be in a better situation than she was. She didn't want to see me struggle like she did. Only God knew what was going to happen to her because it was more than she could bear. My mother was in the hospital a week before for congestive heart failure before she passed away. The doctors said it was okay for her to come home. It was devastating for me to see her lying in bed lifeless. My world went upside down from that point. My mother didn't even get a chance to find out that I was graduating because I was struggling in my math class. At that moment, I wished I would've stayed at home with her instead of going to school.

The judge at the time was my cousin Averen Green, and the apartment managers from the apartments we were evicted from came to witness and sign over on her death certificate. The coroner ruled it as a heart attack. Later that day, the apartment manager of our old apartments collected money for me from everyone in the apartments to show their condolences. My mother had been sick since '93. However, her lungs had gotten worse, and they had put her on oxygen because she was diagnosed with emphysema. Emphysema caused her not to be able to walk far because she had difficulty breathing, so she had to be in a wheelchair if she had to walk somewhere far. We didn't have any transportation at the time, so I had to ride my bike around town to go shopping and get her medicine. Sometimes my uncle or relatives would take me to the store to help me and my mother.

I felt like I had lost my best friend. I cried uncontrollably. My cousin Letha and a few classmates helped console me. I remember calling my father. Everything was silent over the phone. My father came to get me, but my cousin Nancy said that I could stay with her until I graduated. My cousin Cory also wanted me to stay with him. However, I stayed with my cousin Nancy for the last two months. Nancy and my mother were cousins, but they were more like best friends. Nancy and Lee are my godparents; they made sure that I stayed grounded and finished school. I graduated from Bay City High School. All of my relatives came to support me on that night. It was a rainy day but a joyous occasion. I remember waiting in the hallway with the rest of my classmates, waiting to see if we were going to have the ceremony indoors or outdoors on the football field. We decided that we would rather have our graduation out on the field despite the rain. We were all glad and excited that we got to celebrate our last moment in high school on the football field. On the field, we were able to dance across the stage and come across the stage screaming.

When I came across the stage, I was full of joy and tears, thanking the Lord that I had graduated and holding my diploma up high for my mother to see that her daughter had graduated. That year we had lost two classmates to tragic car accidents during prom night; the whole class was filled with mixed emotions. We honored our classmates who had passed. At that moment, I felt like there were three angels watching down on us. It was pouring down rain. I felt my mother's presence after my graduation; I know she was proud of me. During the summer of '99, I left Bay City and went to Prairie View A&M University in the fall. That is where I met my future husband and the father of my children.

Chapter 5

Going to Prairie View A&M University

I remember the day I was leaving for Prairie View A&M University. I was so excited and was wondering what my first day on campus would be like. My father and stepmother were with me on my first day on campus. I had to go to orientation, arrange my class schedule, and wait for the dormitory room to be assigned, which was a long wait, but I had finally gotten my room. I was assigned to Drew Hall. I was the first one in the room. My father and stepmother helped arrange my room. My stepmother told me some stories about her time at Prairie View. We were waiting to meet my roommates. I had to share my room with two roommates, and we had to share a bathroom with three other students. They were our suitemates.

My roommates were from Lubbock and Houston. Tasha was from Lubbock, and she would sing her butt off all the time. She could sing like Mariah Carey. She was cool. Brandi was from Houston, and she became my best friend. She greeted me the moment I saw her. She was smiling and happy. She had a bubbly personality, and she was always upbeat. As I got a chance to know Brandi even more, I learned that she loves the Lord, and the Lord helped us to be close friends so I could stay in church, like my mother did when she was living. Brandi and I joined the school choir called BSM together, which was known as the Baptist Student Movement. I loved being in that choir because we grew spiritually by ministering to other people in college and learning from other people's testimony.

From the day you are born, your parents are telling you to go to college and get your education. You feel like going to college will solve all your problems in the world. However, college is more than just getting your degree. You have a chance of living your life on your own, and you're making all of your decisions on your own. You may face many temptations and challenges that might deter you from getting your degree. However, you should never give up. Always focus on what made you determined to come to college: Was it your lifestyle? Are you the only one in your family who was able to go to college? Or was it the only way to see yourself succeeding in order to provide for yourself in the future? I didn't realize how God had already planned out my journey. We always say and talk about how He always knows what is in our future, but we don't realize it until after we are finished with our goals.

God had prepared me to be around people who serve and love Him; He made sure that I was involved and placed with Christian roommates each year. My sophomore year was the year when I shared my room with a Christian sorority. We had to represent ourselves in a godly way; a lot of things that some of the students were doing on campus were not permitted in our room or off campus. The Lord knew that I would be deterred because I was on the right path, but with a test and trial, I shall learn. That is when I realized that the person I was going to meet as my boyfriend would be my test, and eventually he became my husband.

Chapter 6

The Challenges in My Relationship before Getting Married

Before I got married to my husband, we went through a lot of challenges in our relationship. There was the dating stage, the stage of how long we were going to be in a relationship without being married, and knowing if the person you are dating is the marrying type. I first met my husband at the baby dome in the summer of my sophomore year. I needed help finding my gym class. He and his friend Daniel were going to class, and my husband, Cedric, was walking around me, looking at me with a smile. He asked me if I needed help, and I said yes. We had the same class together. After class, I didn't think I would see him again at my apartment that was on campus. He was knocking on my door, asking for the CA and if I knew where he was. I told him that I didn't know. Then he asked me why I was looking at him in a funny, mean way. I told him that I was just shocked to see him again and wondering why he was knocking at my door. I was just being cautious. He said something to me that made me laugh; from there, we became close. He stayed right upstairs from me. We were always together, studying together. I met most of his friends and his mother when we went on our first date together at the movies.

One day I opened up to him about my mother and how I was missing her. He told me not to grieve but to always remember her. He opened up to me about the relationship between him and his mother and how he doesn't know his father. He just knows of him, and that his father's name is Daniel Hytche. His father left his mother when he was a baby, and the last time he saw him was when he was seven. His father had brought him a bike and talked to him on the phone. His father didn't manage to tell his mother that he was married when they were together. His mother was pregnant with him, and his father told her to have an abortion. Cedric's mother found out he was married through a letter she had found written by his wife asking him to come back home. Unbeknownst to Cedric's mother, Daniel's wife was pregnant at the same time as her. His decision can be perceived as him wanting to go back to his wife for her and his new coming child.

This incident that his father caused left unbroken pieces in my husband's heart. He carried this burden through his childhood and adult life, not feeling loved by a man who was his biological father and having a torn relationship with his mother. He didn't realize that his mother loved him and wanted him to be born because of her faith in the Lord since she was being deceived. He loves her very much and doesn't fault her at all. His father chose to disown him because of the sin he committed. This is why I'm writing this book: to help people and myself learn how to break the cycle from hindrances, abuses, sickness, and many other burdens that can keep us trapped in the past and prevent us from reaching our potential. We should never let our past dictate our future; we shall overcome it.

It was in our relationship that struggles caused him to be so much like his father without even knowing. We had trials of being together. However, God wanted us to stay together. Before I met him, I had seen him in my dream, waiting for me on the steps of a building, but I couldn't understand what it all meant at the time. God was showing me a vision of Cedric in my life and that I would be assigned to him to help him for a moment. I was supposed to grow and learn from the relationship I was in and to help him become a better man. Also to help him find his father so Cedric could at least tell him that he still became a man God called him to be. Even though his father committed adultery and his son came from that sin, his father still had a duty to provide for his child and ask God for forgiveness for the sin he had committed toward him. At the beginning of my book, in chapter 2, I spoke about why my parents got divorced. It can be a never-ending cycle. That cycle can be broken if we choose to learn and study God's words to use it as a guide in life.

We have tried on many occasions to reach out to his father. His father comes from a prominent family and a very educated background. His father's brother, Dr. William Hytche, works at one of the top HBCU colleges, Tennessee State University. It's a shame because I see the resemblance in the family. I have gotten in contact with someone who knew my husband's father, but they hung up on me before I could find out who I was talking to on the phone. I didn't even have a chance to explain who I was or explain the nature of the call. I had to leave a voicemail expressing my emotions because, in the end, you have to confront and repent. I didn't want to leave a message on the voicemail because it was too personal and too many people were involved. I went ahead and left a message because I felt like it was my last chance of getting any contact with his father.

We are hoping that he is still alive because life waits for no one. I don't know what kind of man he is, but so far he is not showing good character. It takes courage to reach out to a person you don't even know. I had to tell my children that they do have another grandfather, and they might never get a chance to meet him. However, in the future, you have to be careful who you meet as a girlfriend or wife because it could be one of his relatives, and you might be related to them. Before my husband's grandmother passed, she wanted me to try to find him and gave me some information so I could help my husband find his father.

His father's family has been staying close by for years, knowing about Cedric and never trying to reach out to him. The sad part is Cedric was the innocent party in the act. Most of the actions my husband took in his life are a reflection of not having a father there to show him how a man is supposed to carry himself as a God-fearing and outstanding man. However, God made his mother strong, and she did an outstanding job in raising him. God never left his side and brought him out of a lot of things. It took me a while to go through with the mission of finding his father because my husband felt like he was okay without knowing at the time as he was looking out for the welfare of Daniel's wife. He said he didn't know what their situation was. He felt like he was caught in the middle of his mother's and father's infidelity. He didn't want to cause any turmoil or friction in his father's marriage because he understood that he was married. However, now that we have children together, we need to know who he is for the sake of my children and our future grandchildren. Deep down in my husband's heart, he still wants to know who he is.

Through the years, we had our own trials. Before we were even married, we had both our children. We always knew we wanted to be together, but we were not ready for marriage. From my point of view, I always wanted to marry him because we knew each other's background and could relate to each other. I also wanted to seek favor in the Lord because God favors marriages. I also didn't want to continue living my life with him and our children and not b married. We were always there for each other. We went through t' same problems most marriages go through. We faced financial pr lems, infidelity, even physical and verbal abuse. A marriage wil' and become strong if you're willing to pray and fight for it with together. Never seek advice outside of your marriage or cou that is not of God, unless it is from your pastor. Go to C External advice can sometimes be wrong, especially if it is ing you stay together and grow spiritually.

Only you know if you have more than you can b of marriages, people lack communication, trust, and l these marriages are not put together by God. A lot o' put together because of benefits, and how can we b relationship? Your spouse needs to know the Lord a In order to have a healthy marriage, you need to b and know how to give unconditional love. That's inside us. If people are in love with Him first being that is in flesh, we will know how to lov'

PROPHETESS EVANGELIST GODIENT A. KELLY-DERBIGNEY

When you stay in a marriage with love, you are winning your fight against the devil and people who don't want to see you have a prosperous marriage. You have proven you really can stay through better or worse, through sickness and health, richer or poorer, and "until death do us part." You have honored your vows. God will favor you and give you blessings. When you keep leaving your spouse and household, you are just leaving more room for Satan to destroy your marriage. When you are not together, there is more room for outsiders to tempt you/her to commit adultery. If you have children, there is a lack of respect for the parent who left because you are showing that you have a problem with commitment and making a change within yourself. If your spouse has forgiven you on more than one occasion and you keep returning with no change in your character, are taking advantage of them. Their forgiveness is not for you; it them and for God to forgive them of their sins. It is not a weakforgive someone because you are able to move on without any your heart, and you can live a healthy, productive life.

meone is bringing toxicity to a relationship, such as being their words and being physical, they will eventually ur well-being. You have to love yourself and can't lose one who doesn't love or know how to love you. Your ve the same problems in their relationship or marmost, we need to go back and reference God's an event in our life. When you feel lost and we need to talk to the Lord and ask Him for o ask Him to send you a sign/message. We re not perfect. Everyone has a purpose. s. Before we are able to do our duties, tribulations. If you haven't experiminister to someone that you have ienced some of the same things, from it?

carry ourselves and treat our ess—forgiveness from our If someone seeks forgivesed against you, you have to find it in your heart and push all pain away to forgive them. You have to forgive people for God to forgive you. God forgives us all the time, no matter how many times we have fallen and how many times we have asked Him to forgive us because He loves us and we know not what we do. He is a forgiving God. Do what God wants you to do and think about what He will do. He wants you to keep forgiving because He will keep forgiving. You don't know how many times you will fall, like the song "We Fall Down (Get Back Up Again)" by Donnie McClurkin.

Chapter 7

Surviving on Our Own and Facing Real-Life Consequence at Prairie View A&M University

During my junior year at Prairie View, I had gotten in trouble with the RN resident director, who is responsible for the students to make great progress while in school. I wasn't allowed to have my husband in my room (he was my boyfriend at the time). I had to make a decision: either get him out of my room so I could stay in my room, or get evicted off campus. I felt at the time I was making a choice for love, and I felt that if it wasn't for him allowing me to stay in his room, I wouldn't be in school. The situation could have turned around where it was me being kicked out of his room. So I decided to move off campus so I could still finish my spring semester. We stayed in Prairie View Inn. Then we moved into a duplex that was rented by my friend's uncle. He let us stay there for $150 a month.

We eventually moved out and had to stay with a friend. Instead of going back home, we had to live with someone who had a drug-dependency disorder. It is sad to be upfront, but we had to live in a crack house. To be truly honest, when we lived there, he had compassion and heart. He even talked to us about going back to school the whole time we were staying with him. I had tried to go back home at that point. It was getting hard and we had to survive some things that might not be approved of by our parents, but we had to step out on our own. I even drove back to Houston because I was tired of struggling and I wasn't able to go back to school at that time. So I decided to go back home, but when I returned, no one answered the door. From then on, I had learned that you have to make it on your own, and you can't turn to anyone because I felt I had to deal with the decision that I had made instead of staying on campus and thinking about what was best for me.

Being able to go to college is once in a lifetime for some people, and for some individuals, going to college wasn't a priority. Not because they didn't think it wasn't important but because achieving a higher education takes financial funding besides financial aid. Furthermore, financial aid back then didn't cover every cost to continue your education. You are most likely left with having to get a job. That is what I have done my junior year. I have worked and went to college. Some people might feel academically that their grades are not appealing for some universities to attend. That is why I speak highly of the universities that do allow students to be admitted into their college with a 2.0. That gives a student a chance to prove to themselves that they can improve their GPA; they just need encouragement and discipline in their study habits.

College is a good influence and can turn any person into a great scholar. Living in a small town around Prairie View without your parents' help left us to depend on each other. We had to do things that our parents might not approve of, but we had to make it out there. The Lord was with us, and that kept us from getting too involved in things that we shouldn't be doing. I got tired, so I drove back to Prairie View and tried to go back to school. I went back to enroll for the next semester, but I wasn't able to attend because I was informed that I had owed money for not finishing the semester. When I found out I was pregnant, I had moved back to Houston and gotten an apartment for me and my firstborn son.

Chapter 8

Breaking the Cycle and a Journey to My Breakthrough

During the time I was separated from my husband, I noticed that I started to break a cycle. My cycle was being abused, experiencing jealousy, being controlled, being hindered, and going back to the same result. No matter what level of abuse it was, it is still abuse. I didn't want my children to suffer because of the love that I had for them. Your children will always love both parents and protect the one who is being hurt. Never have your children in a situation where they have to choose to protect you. Children should never see you fighting because it brings questions into their minds: Do they even love each other? Fighting can be a negative teaching tool and can be a bad influence on their behavior. Children need positive interaction between the parents who love them.

My oldest son asked me this himself one day when we were arguing. "Why does my father act the way he does?" he asked. I responded, "He had to learn from other men who were not his father. He had positive role models in his life, but he doesn't make the right decisions sometimes." I realized now that the majority of the time, I was wrestling with a spirit, not flesh and blood. I felt sometimes he was very dominant and jealous when it came to me wanting to go back to school.

There was an incident when we were on our way to HCC to get him enrolled. He was furious that I wanted to stop at a store located in the same property as the school to get something to drink for the children because we were riding around in a car that had no AC in the middle of summer in Houston. It gets very hot in Houston. My children were young. He got so mad that he threw all of my important paperwork for school out of the car. He was telling me that I didn't want to help him with getting enrolled in school when that wasn't the case. It was about the children, and they come first when it is one hundred degrees outside. HCC was right there on Ella, in the same parking lot.

One day, when I was getting ready to go to work, I and my ex-husband had gotten in an argument. He told me he was going to kill me; he choked me and tried to drown me in the tub. When I ran away from him, someone asked me if I needed a ride, then without thinking, I got in the car. But the devil was around the corner in the car that I had gotten in. The person started talking crazy, and the door latches were missing. I didn't know what happened, but I was able to get out of the car. I was supposed to go to work that day, but I didn't.

This event in my life taught me to slow down when arguing with someone because Satan is busy. All I wanted was to go to work, and an argument started. He was watching from the heavenly realms and listening to the argument. He saw that I was in distress and made a drastic decision that could cause me, my life, and my freedom. I could have been raped or killed.

Arguing with a person could cause you your life or that person to regret what you argue. It can leave you feeling remorseful. Sometimes, the argument can be over something simple. That is why I don't start arguments and try to defuse the argument to keep it from escalating. I always treat my people right. I feed them when they are hungry. If they ask for money, I give it to them; if they need rest/shelter, I will provide them with a place to stay. I don't deny a person when they are in need. It could be their last moment or meal. God just asks us to be wise and give in private (Matthew 6:2–4).

Furthermore, never say what you have done for a person. God has angels in place, and they are released out in the clouds by God. Somewhere, they're in the midst, and you could be speaking to an angel. God asks us to be kind. Kindness kills evil, and forgiveness heals.

He also tried to make me jealous with his past relationships and side relationships he had while we were married. Women called me, just like what happened to my mother. One day I decided to let my kids see their father on Father's Day. He had received a call at the time; he was asking for forgiveness from me and his children, that he didn't mean the things that he did. However, he continued to let a woman call him on Father's Day. I told her, if he is with you, he is calling himself to come back to his children. I know how women can play games sometimes and act like they didn't know he was married, or they ignore that the man they are involved with is married because they do it as they don't have any values. So I told her in front of him that they were playing with fire because God knows that I tried to obey my vows to him. I can't allow him to continue to come back into our children's lives, so he can do what he wants and be adulterous.

He didn't take the marriage seriously, and he didn't stay committed to the Lord. He humiliated me in front of my family and his family. I felt like I wasn't enough for him, and every time we faced financial problems, he would make the situation worse by putting all the financial problems on me. We both worked in the marriage, but I was working the majority of the time more and was responsible when it came to paying the bills and budgeting our finances. I had worked the majority in the relationship. A lot of the things I did for us, I did to support him and to encourage him, not to emasculate him. When you go through financial problems, you are supposed to support and encourage each other through your hard times.

Your relationship can be like a roller coaster, but it has a lot of excitement and good times in it. Whatever it took for me to pay the bills, I worked extra hours at work and also went back to college. I had to hold a promotion sign for the apartments to bring in new residents. Until someone named Janice Sanders Laws, who at the Beverage Stop who used to work for the DA office in Houston, needed to hire an employee for her store. She saw me holding a sign for the apartments that we were living in and decided to take a chance on hiring me. She told her friend who was riding with her, "I should hire her because if she can stand outside holding an advertising sign, she will be a hard worker." Come to find out, her friend was a retired detective from Precinct 7. I was so glad that God sent Ms. Janice Sanders to me. I could have let my pride get in the way, but I didn't. God made sure my family had a stable place to stay. I felt like at the time my husband wanted to just take care of himself and not his family that he created. In a marriage, it is not just about you, especially when you have children. You have to sacrifice the things that you want in order for you to get the things that you need. When a husband puts away his wife, he is leaving her in financial ruin. Some women for their first time have to rely on government assistance to take care of their family. Being on government assistance can have a negative stigma. However, when a man leaves his family for selfish needs, he also leaves them to be blessed. The women learns to be self-sufficient and gains strength to take of her children. A single woman is strong and carries many burdens. She manages to be an overcomer. Many women are placed in high position to show that they are needed, capable of working and can be the head of the household. When the women is married, she is usually not working or only working when needed. The husband should be the sole provider, but when he leaves the woman, she does not know how to keep the family together because she never worked. While in the marriage, she is abiding by the word and letting her husband be the head of the household. Some men can take on sloth, which can look like characteristics of laziness. It is going like spiritual goodness shunning out God. If the men are not working, it leads to poverty.

> Through slothfulness the roof deteriorates, and a house leaks because of idleness. (Ecclesiastes 10:18)

The house falls apart when the man is not working. He needs to stay motivated when not working and create positive work for himself if needed. He doesn't need to stay idle.

> Hardworking hands gain control, but lazy hands do slave labor. (Proverbs 12:24)

In order to stay married, you have to make time for each other to keep the love and spice in the relationship. Always support each other in your achievements and never get jealous because you can do the same as the other person. It is your blessing together because you are married under matrimony to be prosperous together. When you help each other in your goals and better yourselves, you are letting your harvest grow, which is your family. You also have to be as one when it comes to raising the children together. Come to a mutual agreement and never go against each other when you discipline the children. Don't compare your spouse to your parents because you are your own person. You shouldn't have to feel like you have to compete with your in-laws to get approval from your spouse.

I had to teach my children to always love their father and respect him still despite what happens because I don't need them to hold any hard feelings toward him. One day my children will be someone's husband and father. They will need to know how to control their anger and how to speak to their spouse without hurting each other and their feelings. As parents, you shouldn't talk negatively about the other parent to your children just because you're not getting along with the other spouse. Your children will see no wrong and love both parents. God will put forth what needs to be known about the other parent to the children in due time. As parents, we have to understand that children need to keep a positive relationship with both parents so when they get older, they will have less dysfunction in their relationships. You also don't want to ruin your relationship with your children because they might feel differently from what you feel.

Always have a godly approach when you have to talk to your children when you are facing separation, divorce, or even hard times in your household. When people do things that are not of God, you should pray for them so they can change. In order for me to be grounded in the Lord's Word, I had to remove myself from a situation that was not letting me grow. My children and I had to live in a shelter, hotels, and live temporarily at family homes. I was laid off from a job as a security officer. It was getting frustrating for my children because they are used to having a place to stay and the freedom to play and be kids. However, when you are staying in a shelter, you have rules that you have to abide by; and when you are staying with someone, you try to stay out of the way and try not to be a burden.

I started getting closer to God and receiving His Word. I started to go to church more, praying and talking directly to Him—also applying His Word when He comes to me and in the Bible. I started being more obedient to His Word. I already knew the Lord and had a relationship with Him. I even raised our children knowing Him and teaching them to live for Him. When you are going through things in your life, you will have a better understanding and relationship with God. I was at my spiritual growth and breakthrough. When you are at your breakthrough, that is when you have challenges, but you will overcome them because God wants to see you receive your breakthrough. He will send you messages to help you.

I was attending Assembly of God one Sunday morning, and the pastor was speaking to me. I didn't receive it at that time. He was ministering and telling me, "Your breakthrough is here. Don't let anyone seize your harvest. It is yours—claim it." Some of us don't realize that we have been harvesting and working. Then there are some people who will say, "Lord, I have been working faithfully. Why have I not been receiving the things that I want?" God has a way of doing things, and some people are not ready or willing to get to a destination in life to reap their blessings. Sometimes when you are not expecting a blessing, that is when He will pour down blessings in your favor. I sought a healthy lifestyle. I had answered my calling to be a prophetess Evangelist from God; He wanted me to lead the people with His word and to take them out from under false preaching. I became a songwriter and wrote Gospel songs for other upcoming artists. I'm a published writer of four books; *Breaking the Cycle, a Journey to My Breakthrough* will be my first published book. I have a church and ministry called A House of Worship Ministry and a radio podcast show called *Start Now, Talk Now*. Get ready to listen on Spotify. I have another podcast show named *Ministry and Prophetic Messages* by Prophetess Evangelist Godient Kelly-Derbigney. I even started an online store. Hopefully, I will be able to open up a store.

Chapter 9

The Key to a Healthy Marriage

The key to a healthy marriage starts when you are a child. Being raised as a believer of the Lord, your child should be brought up under His word and covenant. Your household should be built on His foundation. As a believer in the Lord, you learn that your life is based on God's Ten Commandments. You must apply those Ten Commandments into your life, unless you are a Gentile. Go by faith and not by the law. When you leave childhood, you become an adult. Men should have learned how to keep a healthy marriage from their parents. The man's parents should be married and under God's covenant. That is where he gets the example of being the man of the household. If his father was a positive leader in the home and continues to build his home on God's foundation, your children remember what was taught in their home and apply it to their

During an argument with your spouse, never threaten to leave their home. It's both your home. Satan will create space between you and your spouse. He will intervene in your household you and your spouse made a promise to God to stay together He knows that it is your blessing and he watches how easily give up on their spouse over issues that can be corrected. P to learn that arguing and talking about each other doesn' issue. It creates gossip and further division. If you are to someone else who doesn't want to see you married, th break up your marriage. God wants you to come to Him. God is part of your foundation. Never leave Him out.

When people get married, some individuals use symbolic traditions like tying the bride and groom with a rope; meaning God is that rope tying you together. No one can break that rope. You will have issues that will be left unsolved. Sometimes you think it is better to start over and leave. However, it only proves that you are willing to start another relationship without figuring out the reason why you had problems in your last marriage. You can carry the same issues into the next relationship. If God put your marriage together, you will be more as one. I'm not saying the marriage will be perfect, but the both of you will share the same religious beliefs and should have a personal relationship with God—actually speaking to God, praying, and even fasting.

As a human being, we are not perfect; we have flaws. Is the ·rson you married God-fearing? They should be scared of the con- 1ences when it comes to honoring your vows. The spouse should ·e in God. Is that person the one that God chose for you? Did ·ose for you like He did Hosea? He chose a whorish wife for losea is a prophet whom God used to portray a message ·ce to God's people. God chose a woman named Gomer, hore. He was comparing Himself to a husband whose itted adultery, a metaphor of the covenant between .el. The marriage shows how she will not be faithful as faithful. If Israel is the people of God, how is Gomer thful? She is not going to be faithful because she is dulterous woman. This metaphor lives on with the people rush into marriages without seeking God es come together because of their own reasons or have influence over their decisions. Sometimes rriages like arranged marriages.

Chapter 10

A Second Chance

As I go over the years and how I grew up, I can say that I was blessed to see how my father received a second chance in life. He was able to remarry again a little after my mother passed. I watch him and his wife interact with each other. They always communicated with each other. He shows her love when it is not a holiday. He didn't give up on their marriage when they had marital issues. He fought for her. He learned from his first marriage that marriage is not easy, but if you truly love them, you will try harder to resolve your problems. I received positive influence from them, which taught me that I can be granted a second chance and have a happy, healthy relationship.

My father has helped me and stood by my side. He told me what I needed to hear, not what I wanted to hear. I thank God for letting me understand that people can change. I saw true happiness with my father and stepmother. I watch how they respect each other in front of other people. How they don't make big decisions without the other knowing. How they believe in God and love God. God can bless you in many ways. God blesses you with wisdom, strength, health, mental health, courage, and love.

Allowing your first marriage to past and not be bonded under God is through a passing of a spouse. When you are able to get remarried, it is not adultery. That adultery is your second. You also can get remarried to your first spouse before passing.

Chapter 11

Preach, Reach, and Teach

You have to preach the Word of God to reach your brothers and sisters in the Lord. To seek Him and preach into their spirits to guide others who may not know God and are not serving Him. When you are reaching souls, you are also teaching the individual to stay under His Word to remove themselves from earthly ways. God's Word is our armor and is used as our guide in life. You will often hear people say that we came into this world with no instruction or that they are living according to what life has given them. However, that phrase is untrue. We have been given the Word, and as we live, we should be living the Word of God. His Word needs to be told so people can know about Him and get to know Him intimately. First, His children need to mature spiritually so they can stop living on their own and teaching themselves. Secondly, they need to stop learning from others who have not learned or know the Word of God. Accept their sinful nature and don't judge. Embrace the newcomers with love and forgiveness. That is not much for you to do to save a soul.

In Memory of Vivian L Kelly

My mother was a kind, living spirit who passed on her wisdom and kindness to me. I was able to learn from her testimony and to be delivered in order for me to tell my own testimony. My mother had experienced many forms of adversity from the military, family members, friends, and spouse. However, that helped me to not be ashamed or humiliated by what has happened in my life. The mistreatment didn't keep us from living and gave me the tools to tell our story to give hope and encouragement to others—you can overcome every trial.

As I live on for her, I will always honor my mother. She was Private First Class Vivian Laruth Kelly. Her family is proud of her and will always remember her for her elegance, beauty, laughter, songful voice (always singing the Lord's praises), and her way of telling her family and friends to live your life for you and no one else. My mother was my drill sergeant and prayer worshiper. She gave me all that I needed. May our story help others to see how God works miracles in our lives.

My mother in our apartment in Bay City in '99

My mother's high school picture

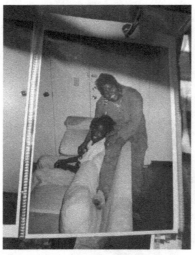

My mother and me at home in the Wheatley Courts in '93

BREAKING THE CYCLE

My mother's army entry pictures

My mother's military burial flag

Giving Thanks

First and foremost, I would like to give thanks to my Heavenly Father for keeping me and preparing me on my journey. In every step of my life, I was not alone; He was the Potter to this clay. I would also like to thank my family and friends for being God-fearing and for showing the love of God in their hearts. They were the light in my life.

I give thanks to my supporters and readers. May *Breaking the Cycle: A Journey to My Breakthrough* bless your homes, encouraging you to stay together with the Lord and letting God be the foundation in your home. Last but not least, I would like to thank Convent Book Publishing for giving me the opportunity to publish my book with them. Many doors were closed, but a window was opened for me. Thank you, everyone.

About the Author

Godient A. Kelly-Derbigney was born in Buffalo, New York, and raised in Texas. During her childhood years, Godient lived in Houston, the east side of San Antonio, and Bay City, a small town near Houston. She was married for nine years and was with her husband for twenty-two years. She and her husband have two sons together.

Godient has been called on to minister, and she uses her writing skills to minister to people all over the world. Godient enjoys writing books and songs and singing Gospel music. She was inspired to write due to her mother, with whom she shared some of the same life experiences. Her mother always wanted to tell her story. However, due to her passing, her daughter Godient decided to share her story, including her own, to reach women, men, or anyone who has been through a cycle of life changes that caused brokenness that only God can heal and fix.

My cousin and me at our ladies' night

My high school graduation picture class of '99 in Bay City High School

Me s leaking at my cousin Tonya's Domestic Violence Gala, October 2023

Mr. Walter's store on the Eastside. Mr. Walter taught me to let my boyfriend pay for whatever I want in the store. Men always pay a lady's bills and take care of her with love.

My middle school Wheatley Middle School. It is now called Young Men's Leadership Academy.

Wheatley Courts Apartments

...tley Courts Apartments' office